Humpty Dumpty had come to the door, the White Queen said,

"because he was looking for a hippopotamus. Now, as it happened,
 there wasn't such a thing in the house, that morning."
"Is there generally?" Alice asked in an astonished tone.
"Well, only on Thursdays," said the Queen.

—LEWIS CARROLL, *Through the Looking Glass*

Our Peaceable Kingdom

Our Peaceable Kingdom

THE PHOTOGRAPHS OF

JOHN DRYSDALE

Compiled and Introduced by Margaret Regan

ST. MARTIN'S PRESS ❧ NEW YORK

The photographs in this book have not been
electronically altered or manipulated.

www.stmartins.com

Design by Kathryn Parise
Edited by Brad Wood

LIBRARY OF CONGRESS CATALOGING-IN-PUBLICATION DATA
Drysdale, John.
    Our peaceable kingdom: the photographs of John Drysdale/compiled
and introduced by Margaret Regan.—1st ed.
        p. cm.
    ISBN 0-312-26588-3
        1. Photography of children. 2. Photography of animals. 3. Children and
    animals—Pictorial works. I. Regan, Margaret. II. Title.
    TR 681.C5 D78 2000
    779'.32—dc21   00-040516

Frontispiece photo: *Thursday*, 1989.
Half-title-page photo and title-page photo: *The Cameraman I/The Cameraman II*, 1992.

First Edition: October 2000

10 9 8 7 6 5 4 3 2 1

CONTENTS

INTRODUCTION

—◦⁓◦—

British photographer John Drysdale's pictures can be deceptive. They seem to depict play—spontaneous fun and funniness, exquisite ease and frolic, the real and the surreal cozily at home in the world together. But we should not forget that play, along with its larkiness and hilarity and glee, is very serious. And that it is civilized and civilizing.

At bottom, Drysdale's pictures reveal the emotion of love. Brimful of play, his guileless subjects luxuriate in strong and happy feeling, in loving and being loved. We see the conventional gestures and natural abandon of love, the ordinary moments of love, but among a most unexpected and extraordinary mix of creatures. Beethoven claimed that next to love, the best things in life are surprises. And John Drysdale's droll and elegant eye revels in surprise. When did *you* last embrace a hippopotamus? And if you have, did you then invite the hippo into your house to watch television? And when did you last notice that your dog was in thrall to, and enthralled by, a llama? Or that your cat had unselfishly befriended a white mouse, even sharing her dish of milk with him?

Whether we gasp and gape, or laugh and laud, we recognize the imperishable longing of the heart—and not just the human heart!—for affection. Pervading the strange and humorous beauty of Drysdale's gaze, of his receptiveness to fleeting moments that enshrine the wit and wildness and tenderness of experience, is the verve of his subjects' affection—affection that is unconstrained and unguarded and unambiguous, untutored and unselfconscious and uncomplicated. And unusual, i.e., unusual to a culture that tends to glorify human romantic love and sometimes forgets the importance, even the existence, of love that flourishes between friends, human and nonhuman. But in the wonderland of John Drysdale, love is various. And love is wise.

Rather than limit love to the commotion of romantic ardor, of being in love, Drysdale's world reminds us that it is smart and helpful to be loving, to forge friendships that make life less difficult for one another, even to play and prance and have fun together. Self-preservation thrives on

calmer aspects of love: empathy, cooperation, and kindness. With pictures that have the deft power to engage our serious reflection and to tickle laughter out of us, that have a sense of beauty and a sense of humor, Drysdale evokes a place of sunlit harmony and mirth, a peaceable kingdom, abounding in delights.

But interspecies love? Between wild and domestic animals and humans? Why ever not? Though Drysdale has pointed his camera at unlikely friends who are bizarrely unalike, we are soon ambushed by a greater surprise: suddenly our attention is spirited away from odd juxtaposition and dissimilarity and magically ushered into a portrait gallery of affinities, where resemblances sparkle and differences fade to insignificance. It is as if one were freed to regard intimacy anew, for, the very strangeness of these friends intensifies the mystery and majesty and emotional power of love. Natural feeling outwits the unnatural. "Curiouser and curiouser," as Lewis Carroll's Alice said. And eminently sane, as John Drysdale and his subjects might say. (A celebration of seeing, one could add.)

Always gracefully composed and eloquent of wonder, each rendering the improbable familiar and the ephemeral momentous, these photographs flare into merriment and gladden us with their unexpected emotional truths. They are the achievement of Drysdale's lifelong alertness to the feelings and personalities of animals and children—since his boyhood in remote regions of Africa, surrounded by wildlife, and despite his many years in the most sophisticated circles of London society. Whether working at Vogue Studios or in Fleet Street, assisting on Condé Nast assignments or in making portraits of the Royal Family at Buckingham Palace, Drysdale would steadfastly return to his animal and children studies, peering at life—at the startling otherness of others—from odd and playful angles.

This watchfulness, very much a reverence, has spawned a body of work that leads us into exotic adventure, at once comic and enlivening and fun, via an agile and generous guide. It is a watchfulness that gives us a peek into the lives of certain beings with whom we share the earth: those who are less noticed, less considered, and who have met and liked and bonded with one another—anomalously or in circumstances unusual, yet with feelings marked by a gift for friendship. With deference and delicacy, Drysdale has slyly brought to light a corner of the world where the ways of the heart are winding and magical as a Venetian canal, and from where he has brought back pictures that exemplify W. B. Yeats's statement, "Only that which does not teach, which does not cry out, which does not persuade, which does not condescend, which does not explain, is irresistible."

—Margaret Regan

Swinging High, 1972

Bulldog Watch, 1969

Just Looking, 1975

After Lunch, 1989

Frinton-on-Sea, 1988

Bookworms, 1974

Descending a Staircase, 1976

Bath Time, 1976

Patience of a Saint, 1970

Special Delivery, 1990

Full Speed, 1969

Caught Reading, 1991

My Greatest Friend, 1986

Puppy-Loving Chimp, 1970

In Harness, 1970

Baking Day, 1969

Soda Sippers, 1989

Odd Girl Out, 1965

Peekaboo, 1990

Ear Nibble, 1967

Back to Back, 1967

The Duet, 1967

Footloose, 1978

Hat Thief, 1987

Wee Wallaby, 1991

Bearing the Brunt, 1975

Gone Fishing, 1976

Dog Goalie, 1955

Tennis, Anyone? 1967

Baring the Teeth, 1975

Great-Grandfather and Baby, 1994

Wolf Cubs and Kid, 1994

No Evil, 1974

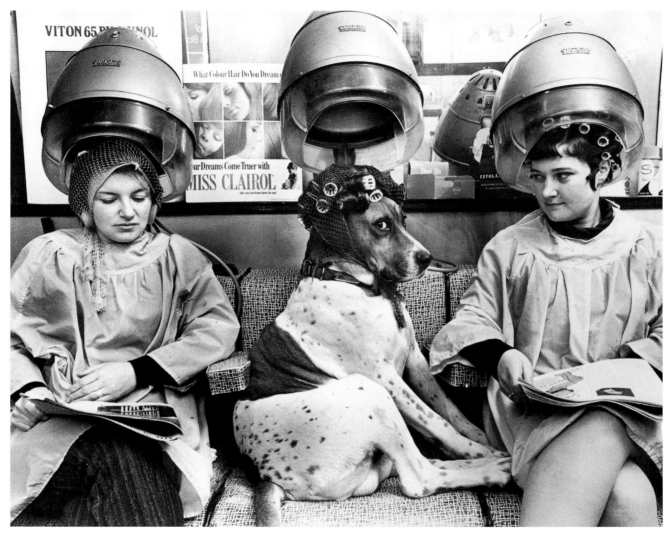

Canine Coiffure, 1969

Boston Terrier Laugh, 1992

Sharing, 1970

Lion and Little Friend, 1973

Chick on Chimp, 1992

Street Pedallers, 1956

Flat Ball, 1956

Formal Introduction, 1981

The Chauffeur, 1974

Duck and Tiger Cub Snuggle, 1978

Embraceable You, 1985

Rearing Up, 1973

Three Ostriches, 1975

Friend of the Danes, 1970

Big Dog, Little Dog, 1992

Cat Pounce, 1972

Pub Stop, 1974

First Steps, 1958

Honey, 1958

Bikers, 1989

Market Day, 1996

Tiger Dive, 1975

Out on the Lake, 1984

Cubs in Boots, 1975

Baby Triplets, 1965

Twilight in Paddington, 1956

Afternoon Chat, 1958

Billy Goat and Mouse, 1981

Clinging, 1969

Follow the Leader, 1975

Follow Her, 1989

Cozy Cat, 1981

Black Cat on Cobblestones, 1954

The Strut, 1958

Sword Fight, 1956

There, There . . . , 1972

The Lecture, 1975

Comfort of Friends I, 1994

Comfort of Friends II, 1979

A Quick Bite, 1998

Pelican Speech, 1967

Out for a Walk I, 1993

Out for a Walk II, 1994

Swan Nestling on German Shepherd, 1994

Duck's Fun, 1989

The Début, 1970

Big Man, Little Man, 1970

82 **Washerwomen, 1979**

Baby in a Tub, 1969

Snug, 1979

The Secret, 1972

A Musical Itch, 1969

Lamppost Swing, 1958

The Kiss, 1994

Seaside, 1998

In the Piggery I and II, 1975

Regal Profile, 1994

Cat Nap, 1970

Cub Cuddle, 1973

Hand in Hand, 1989

NOTES ON SELECTED
PHOTOGRAPHS

Thursday, 1989 (*frontispiece*)
The young hippopotamus was attacked by a male hippo and removed for safety. After a difficult period being bottle-fed, the baby hippo roamed freely in the garden and would enter the house, hoping for more food and sometimes watching television with the little boy. The boy and the hippo were hugely amused by each other.

The Cameraman I/The Cameraman II, 1992 (*pages ii and iv*)
The red-tailed hawk at the Earl of Bradford's Weston Park home participated in free-flying displays and knew that the falconer always stored meat under a black cloth. In a case of mistaken identity, the hawk assumed there was meat under an architectural photographer's focusing cloth.

Swinging High, 1972 (*page 1*)
Two joyful four-year-olds have fun together in the garden. The chimpanzee was raised in the family and was like a sibling to the little girl.

Bulldog Watch, 1969 (*page 2*)
Suzie the bulldog's puppies had recently been sold when someone brought three tiny gray squirrels to the farm where she lived, near Southam, England. Assuming they had been abandoned by their mother, the farmer undertook the laborious task of feeding the frail little squirrels with a syringe every two hours. He then successfully transferred nursing to Suzie, whose strong maternal instincts welcomed and protected them. As the squirrels recovered and began growing normally, they accepted the bulldog as their mother and seemed domesticated by her. Meanwhile, Suzie of the fearsome look and gentle nature was happy in her mothering role, and she was revivified—no longer forlorn over the loss of her puppies.

Just Looking, 1975 (*page 3*)
When a poultry farmer found a tiny fox cub exhausted and near death in a field, he brought it home and fed it raw eggs and milk through a syringe until it was healthy and strong. The fox grew up to become the family pet. But first it had to become familiar with and respectful of the family's business—duck rearing. The fox adapted and lived like a family dog, following the farmer on his rounds in the duck enclosures and casting a protective eye on the ducklings.

After Lunch, 1989 (*page 4*)
The chimp had to be removed from a colony on a lake island when she could no longer bear social fighting within the group. She settled happily into human family life, even enjoying the comfort of her own miniature deck chair.

Frinton-on-Sea, 1988 (*page 5*)
The macaw and the man lived next to the beach, at Frinton-on-Sea, England, and had been together for forty years.

Bookworms, 1974 (*page 6*)
The miniature donkey lived the life of one highborn: instead of a damp, windy stable, she delighted in the velvety comforts of the sitting room with her close friend.

Descending a Staircase, 1976 (*page 7*)
Admiral Horatio Nelson lived in this baronial hall in Cricket St. Thomas, England, and walked up and down this staircase two centuries before the little girl used it to exercise her father's pet crocodile.

Bath Time, 1976 (*page 8*)
During his nightly bath, the little boy, Jeremy, was routinely visited by lion cub Kitty, who had needed bottle-feeding and grew up in the household—with five dogs and a dingo. Jeremy seemed to regard them all as dogs. His father suspected that the lion also thought of herself as a dog. Dogs, dingo, lion, and Jeremy played happily together, and all went on long walks in the surrounding Welsh mountains.

Special Delivery, 1990 (*page 10*)
A chicken farmer who used to make egg deliveries in a horse and cart decided to build a miniature egg wagon that could be pulled in harness by a certain free-range hen, who had formed an attachment to him and who always followed him about on his daily rounds. The eccentric idea was successful. After gathering the eggs, the farmer would load them into the little cart, and the hen would deliver them along a two-hundred-yard footpath to the back door of his home.

Full Speed, 1969 (*page 11*)
The lambs were bottle-fed by a Cornish farmer and became playmates for his daughters. When they grew into sheep, the girls enjoyed a few gentle rides, which eventually developed into full-tilt galloping.

Caught Reading, 1991 (*page 12*)
At Kerbymoorside, Yorkshire, both seemed absorbed utterly.

My Greatest Friend, 1986 (*page 13*)
The girl grew up with the elephant and they became best friends, playing with one another daily. They simply liked being together, and, since the elephant had the unusual ability to sit on his haunches, they were able to be close with physical ease.

Puppy-Loving Chimp, 1970 (*page 14*)
The affectionate chimpanzee grew up in the friendly company of several Jack Russell terriers, and even grew fond of their puppies.

In Harness, 1970 (*page 15*)
Resembling a junior Santa Claus with his Rein-dogs, the baby was actually a convenient hitching post for the dogs returning from a walk, while his mother was closing the gates.

Baking Day, 1969 (*page 16*)
A gray-headed fish eagle at Lord Masereen's mansion near Canterbury, England, considered one of the few large birds to fly indoors, exploits the cook's inattention and filches a freshly cracked egg.

Odd Girl Out, 1965 (*page 18*)
The first day of school can be confusing, and full of distractions.

Ear Nibble/Back to Back, 1967 (*pages 20 and 21*)
The orphaned llama and the Rhodesian Ridgeback became fast friends and played and stayed together day and night.

The Duet, 1967 (*page 22*)
In a Welsh mansion, a lioness is in her glory whenever her mistress plays the piano.

Footloose, 1978 (*page 23*)
When asked by his mother to lend a hand with the tedious task of holding a feeding bottle several times a day, the boy devised an ingenious bit of footwork to accomplish the job and to remain free to focus on more boyish concerns.

Wee Wallaby, 1991 (*page 25*)
A tiny, hairless wallaby was found scarcely alive inside its dead mother's pouch. Fed by syringe, it survived and became the little girl's friend.

Bearing the Brunt, 1975 (*page 26*)
Bogged down in thick mud, the two men received unexpected help via the great weight of a European brown bear, whom they knew and with whom they were on friendly terms, but whose altruism might have been roused by the tempting load of apples they were transporting.

Gone Fishing, 1976 (*page 27*)
Because people routinely take their dogs fishing, the man wondered why anyone would think it peculiar for him to take along his child and his elephant, both of whom loved angling outings.

Dog Goalie, 1955 (*page 28*)
In London, certain streets were once designated as "play streets" and were closed to traffic. Though the goal-posts in this play street were entirely imaginary, the dog and a small group of boys were engaged in a stirring football game, with the dog being treated as an equal player and acting as goalkeeper. He was such a skilled goalie that none of the boys were able to score.

Tennis, Anyone?, 1967 (*page 29*)
Having a cavernous mouth, and thereby having developed the knack of fielding two balls, the Great Dane became an ideal "ball boy" during her owners' tennis matches.

Great-Grandfather and Baby, 1994 (*page 31*)
Another century will pass before the baby Seychelles tortoise, weighing little more than a cabbage leaf, reaches the size of Goliath, who is estimated to be 115 years old.

Canine Coiffure, 1969 (*page 34*)
The owner of a London hair salon always brought his Labrador-mastiff, Rex, to work—and Rex always sat on any chair not occupied. Through the years, the regular customers thought it perfectly normal, routine, to find Rex seated beside them. But people new to the salon were always asking why a dog was sitting under the dryer. And so the owner fashioned a hairnet and curler wig for Rex. Now, when anyone was particularly pesky on a busy day, persistently questioning the seating preferences of Rex, the owner would whip out the wig, pop it on the dog's head, and he and Rex would look at the customer as if to say—Why do you *think* he's sitting there? Obviously, to prove that he can look as ridiculous as humans do.

Boston Terrier Laugh, 1992 (*page 35*)
The shy and gentle Boston terrier, inappropriately named "Bossy," was constantly being harassed by rough, neighboring dogs near his home in Oundle, England. When his mistress was asked to bottle-feed an abandoned lion cub, she brought it to Bossy for company. They became close friends, and Sylvia, the lion cub, became very protective of the Boston terrier. The aggressive dogs in the district gave the pair a wide berth, and Bossy, at last free of their torment and happy with his beloved Sylvia, would now often smile and laugh.

Sharing, 1970 (*page 36*)
When a boy brought home a little white mouse from school, his mother explained that theirs was not a suitable house for a mouse; their cat was a terror to birds, and a mouse would fare no better. But the mouse escaped and ran past the cat, who did not stir. Cautious experiment proved that the devil with birds was an angel with mice, and the cat and mouse became inseparable friends.

Chick on Chimp, 1992 (*pages 38 and 39*)
When the five-year-old chimpanzee was shown a day-old chick, he was intrigued. He carefully held it on his finger before gently placing it on his stomach, holding it aloft on his foot, and finally letting it flutter onto his head.

Street Pedallers, 1956 (*page 40*)
A classic pedal car speeds along an inner London street, thrilling the three boys. Their play streets were closed to traffic.

Flat Ball, 1956 (*page 41*)
Though the football is flat, the boys' fun is not a jot diminished in this London play street.

The Chauffeur, 1974 (*page 43*)
The expensive miniature donkey, pet of a wealthy family, stylishly arrives at their city home.

Rearing Up, 1973 (*page 46*)
Sharing a lake with a two-ton elephant seal, the sea lions formed a strange partnership: when the elephant seal swam around like a submarine, the wily sea lions would ride on its back in pairs, to save effort. But when the swimming stopped, the sea lions, impatient for a ride and for more fun, would try to coax their elephant-seal–ship back into the water.

Three Ostriches, 1975 (*page 47*)
Seconds after the camera clicked, two birds stepped out from behind the one in front, thereby undoing their tidy queue—and the illusion of a three-headed ostrich.

Friend of the Danes, 1970 (*page 48*)
Five champion Harlequin Great Danes, weighing more than seven hundred pounds, deter intruders and are gentle playmates.

Cat Pounce, 1972 (*page 50*)
Having strayed from the vixen, the fox was found alone in Market Drayton, England. It was rescued and given care, and grew up in a house with many cats, all of whom treated the fox as equal friend and playmate.

Pub Stop, 1974 (*page 51*)
At the pub near Billericay, Essex, the horse had become a steady customer after having shown a liking for beer. The horse grew accustomed to enjoying a pint, and would regularly enter the pub and be served at the owner's expense. The ambience inside the pub was one of nonchalant good fellowship between horse and human patrons.

First Steps, 1958 (*page 52*)
Children's Dancing School, Knightsbridge, London.

Honey, 1958 (*page 53*)
An unhappy bee impatiently awaits his share of the nectar.

Bikers, 1989 (*page 54*)
In Wigston Magna, England, a young woman gives her dog and macaw a ride through the park.

Market Day, 1996 (*page 55*)
After teaching her Lhasa apso dog clever tricks, the woman cleverly encouraged the willing pooch to help with the chores.

Tiger Dive, 1975 (*page 56*)
Tigers love water, and this one could not resist the lure of a pool on a hot day. The other bathers had to avoid her claws.

Out on the Lake, 1984 (*page 57*)
In Rutland, England, the Labrador-collie was not content to wait on the shore and watch her mistress water-skiing. After each ski run, she would swim out into the lake and retrieve her owner's skis, often struggling to get on them herself. Eventually, her mistress tried an experiment: she clamped a board onto the skis to see if they could ski together and if the dog would like it. The dog loved it, every minute of it, and she would bark happily, triumphantly, and continually throughout her water-ski rides.

Clinging, 1969 (*page 63*)
Marmosets have a physical and emotional need to cling to a parent. This orphaned bush baby was comforted by a sweet-tempered Labrador retriever.

Follow the Leader, 1975 (*page 64*)
A bulldog and a five-year-old girl can not resist exploring a hollow log, which the girl's grandfather had just delivered so it could be chopped up for firewood.

Follow Her, 1989 (*page 65*)
To reach the branches of nearby trees, for climbing fun and exercise, two honey bears follow their leader along the top of a wall.

Cozy Cat, 1981 (*page 66*)
The young cat's mother lived in the donkey's stable for many years. The cat had learned to jump from a shelf onto the donkey's back, enjoying its company and its body warmth—and the view and the transportation.

Black Cat on Cobblestones, 1954 (*page 67*)
Rome, Italy. The black cat was en route to a street market near the Forum, where he would filch or beg for food. Like scores of other cats, he lived wild among the ancient ruins, surviving on a chancy mix of mice, market manna, and the mercies of feline-loving Romans.

The Strut, 1958 (*page 68*)
The charms and bearing of an aspiring model captivate neighboring children in a Paddington street.

Sword Fight, 1956 (*page 69*)
Absent conventional toys, dustbin covers and sticks can provide endless fun.

There, There . . . , 1972 (*page 70*)
The five-year-old chimpanzee was badly treated by her own mother, but was later rescued, befriended, and rehabilitated. With a nine-month-old human baby who had begun crying, the tender chimp seemed to know exactly what was needed and provided soothing comfort while the baby's mother prepared a bottle.

Comfort of Friends I, 1994 (*page 72*)
Though raised as a household pet, the basset hound gave up the comforts of life in his owners' home for the spartan environment of the stables, where he had formed a strange and lasting bond with a young camel.

Comfort of Friends II, 1979 (*page 73*)
The young Bactrian camel, uncommonly even tempered and without the usual irritability and quickness to bite, had made friends with the little girl, who enjoyed the comfort of his coat—and her own thumb.

A Quick Bite, 1998 (*page 74*)
The boy's father keeps many tame, free-flying, exotic birds. The macaw seemed to disregard his own feeding times, for, like Oliver Twist, he wanted more.

Out for a Walk I, 1993 (*page 76*)
When out on their daily walk, the boy generally held onto the tail of the cheetah, seeming to know instinctively that because cheetahs move so quickly they require a bit of restraint if a little chap is to keep pace.

Out for a Walk II, 1994 (*page 77*)
As the basset hound spent most of his time following the owner while she tended a large number of horses, all of whom were friendly to the dog, his mistress decided to put him to work. When she led a horse, the dependable dog would follow her, leading another.

Swan Nestling on German Shepherd, 1994 (*page 78*)
A wild mute swan strayed from her territory on the River Thames, in England, and was badly injured and blinded by an attack from other swans. For a wild bird this meant certain death from predators. She was rescued, however, and after treatment at an animal hospital, she was fed by a tube and recovered all but her sight. The swan soon accepted the company—and eventual friendship—of a German shepherd, whom she would follow by scent, using the dog as her eyes. Wearing a specially made harness attached to a long cord, the swan was brought to the river each day for exercise and a swim. She would then be returned to her friend and protector and guide, the German shepherd, on whose back she would happily nestle.

Duck's Fun, 1989 (*page 79*)
To keep it warm in winter, the tortoise was put in a heated cabinet with ducks, who regarded the shell as a convenient perch—and great fun when it was on the move.

The Début, 1970 (*page 80*)
A dance class in Aldwych, London.

Big Man, Little Man, 1970 (*page 81*)
A man walks with his grandson, in Leyton, England.

Washerwomen, 1979 (*page 82*)
The cat, a Persian show champion, was not at her most elegant the day before a competition. After a blow-dry and lavish combing, however, she easily won the silver cup.

Snug, 1979 (*page 84*)
The young Indian elephant was accustomed to and tolerant of free-range hens and their chicks frequenting his territory, searching for scattered seeds. None was ever harmed. One brave little chick, showing especial interest in the elephant, would be put on his back and then scamper to the comforting shelter in the crevice behind his ear. Elephant and chick were perfectly content with this arrangement and with each other.

A Musical Itch, 1969 (*page 86*)
During the performance of her solo part in a youth orchestra, the girl felt an overpowering itch aside her nose, which she quashed with a quick swipe of the bow and with remarkable aplomb, before deftly continuing the piece.

Lamppost Swing, 1958 (*page 87*)
When the street is the playground, an old lamppost serves as a swing for an exuberant boy.

In the Piggery I and II, 1975 (*page 90*)
A tabby cat who gave birth in a barn in Norfolk, England, that housed a sow and eight piglets was taken into the farmer's house for greater comfort. But the cat refused to join the humans and took her kittens back to the barn, preferring the company of pigs. The kittens played with the piglets, and one of them was seen suckling with no objection from the sow. All but one kitten were taken to new homes. But the one pictured remained—and remained friendly with the pigs, even after they had grown considerably larger than their feline playmate.

Hand in Hand, 1989 (*page 94*)
Three little ones, of similar age and size, share common interests.

ABOUT THE PHOTOGRAPHER,
JOHN DRYSDALE

———⟨∞⟩———

Born in Uganda and raised in remote regions then teeming with wildlife, British photographer John Drysdale took his first pictures in Africa, using a 2,000-gallon water tank as his (very hot) darkroom. His father, Kenneth Drysdale, had been one of the first to organize and conduct nonhunting wild animal safaris, in Uganda and Kenya, beginning in 1927. Though he eventually arranged safaris for nearly all the crowned heads of Europe and a succession of Americans—from the Duke of Windsor to the Vanderbilts—a large part of Kenneth Drysdale's work was guiding and advising British and Hollywood filmmakers shooting on location in Africa. Thus the presence and importance of animals and cameras became a regular part of John Drysdale's early life.

Visiting relatives in Surrey, England, John Drysdale received an invitation to study at the Guildford College of Art, noted for its program in photography. His studies completed, he remained in England and worked for many years in London, with Norman Parkinson at Vogue Studios and with Cecil Beaton as court photographer for the Royal Family. His first major assignment was assisting Beaton in photographing all the royals of Europe in Buckingham Palace after the coronation ceremony of Queen Elizabeth II in 1953. Prince Charles and Princess Anne, then small children in high spirits, were running about and had to be repeatedly carried back into the portrait groups—a nightmare, since the royals were roasting under hot lights and needed to "freeze" for pictures, most of which were ruined by excessive movement.

Meantime, Drysdale began photographing unposed children, without royal titles, in the streets of London, and his first successes in Fleet Street were for picture stories of these city scenes. His diverse daily work—including fashion and advertising, portraits of royalty and celebrities, architectural interiors and gardens, and photojournalism—never hindered his studies of children nor lessened his abiding interest in animals, both wild and domestic. He returned to Africa several times to photograph animals in various wildlife areas. In 1992, he visited the primeval wilderness of the Okavango Delta, one of the last truly wild places on earth.

John Drysdale's publishing credits and exhibitions are extensive, and his renown is worldwide, especially for his photographs of unusual interspecies bonding and of children. His awards include prizes from British Press Pictures of the Year and from World Press Photo. He lives in England.